Copyright ©2018 by Diana Rowe.
Library of Congress Number 2018909126

ISBN: Softcover: 978-0-9989420-4-9
EBook: 978-0-9989420-5-6

All rights reserved. No part of this book may be reproduced or transmitted in any form or by any means, electronic or mechanical, including photocopying, recording, or by any information storage and retrieval system, without permission in writing from the copyright owner.

Rev. 07/24/2018

Published by: Lillie of the Vallie
For Additional Copies:
LilliValliePublishing@gmail.com

Unless otherwise stated, scripture quotations are taken from the Holy Bible, NIV.." 1973, 1978, 1984 by the International Bible Society. Used by permission of Zondervan. All rights reserved. [Biblica]

CONTENTS

Letter 4

Bible & Mathematics 5

Bible & ELA 6

Bible & Reading Comp 7

Bible & Reading - Story Structure 8

Bible & Reading - Author's Purpose 9

Bible & Writing 10

Bible Comprehension & Exploration 11

Bible & Science 12

Outreach Evangelism: Blood Drive 13

Bible & Social Studies 14

Outreach Evangelism: Invitation 15

Bible & Arts 16

Inclusive Lesson Plan Format 17

Student Accountability Contract 18

Student Accountability Self-Evaluation 19

Worksheets 20

Graphic Organizer 21

Friendly Letter 22

Business Letter 23

Evangelism Worksheet 24, 25

Educator's Prayer 26

DEAR TEACHERS AND ADMINISTRATORS,

Thank you for all that you do to transform the lives of students and help create a better society. I pray that this planning help will make your day lighter and give you some ideas as you work through the story.

May the Lord be with you as you labor for Him each day. May the Holy Spirit guide you as you plan lessons that will lead students and families into His presence.

Have a tremendously blessed school year.

Faithfully,

Diana Rowe
Author & Fellow Educator

"…And teaching them everything that I have commanded you, and surely I am with you Always, even to the end of the age."
Matthew 28:20 (NIV).

BIBLE & MATHEMATICS IDEAS
GROUP SPECIAL NEEDS STUDENTS WITH ENCOURAGERS

1. Add the length and width of the outer courtyard of the Sanctuary. (Exodus 27: 18).

2. Find the total number of men in the tribes in the camps around the earthly Sanctuary (Numbers 2).

3. What is the difference between the camp of Dan and the camp of Naphtali? (Numbers 2).

4. What is the sum of the tribe of Benjamin, the tribe of Manasseh, and the tribe of Simeon? (Numbers 2).

5. Calculate how many times the high priest would have to enter the Most Holy place from your first birthday to your current age right now.

6. Compare that number (from # 5) to the number of times Jesus entered the Most Holy place on your behalf.

7. Calculate how many animals you would have to sacrifice for sin from your first birthday to your current age now.

8. According to Leviticus 5:7; 6:25; 9:2-3, 7; 12: 6, 8, each individual had to offer a sin offering on the altar and also a guilt offering (Leviticus 5:7, 10, 17-18). Burnt offerings were to be made each day in the morning and in the evening (Exodus 29: 38-42; Numbers 28: 3, 6; 2 Chronicles 2:4).

9. Based on this information, how many sin and guilt offerings would you bring to the altar each week?

10. How many sin and guilt offerings would you bring in a month?

11. How many sin and guilt offerings would you bring in a year?

12. Count the number of people living in your home. Calculate how many sin offering and guilt offering would be offered for each person every month and every year.

13. Determine how many sin offering and guilt offering would be offered for everyone in your home include yourself for one year.

14. How many times was Jesus offered up for the sins of your entire household including you?

15. Think about these numbers. Think about what Jesus did and why it was important for Him to replace all the animals for both sin and guilt.

16. How does this impact your heart about Jesus' love and mercy toward you and your family?

17. Show 10 people who have done something wrong what Jesus has done to remove their sin and guilt. Help them to recognize that God still loves them in spite of their sin.

BIBLE & ENGLISH LANGUAGE ARTS IDEAS

GRAMMAR AND CONVENTIONS TO DEVELOP LISTENING, SPEAKING, AND WRITING. STUDENTS MAY WORK ON PAPER OR TECHNOLOGY EQUIPMENT TO SHARE OR POST ONLINE.

1. Locate 10 declarative sentences in the story. Share in online journal or in class. Explain the context for each use.

2. Locate 5 imperative sentences in the story. Share in online journal or in class. Explain the context for each.

3. Locate 8 interrogative sentences in the story. Share with classmates. Explain the context for each.

4. Locate 8 exclamatory sentences in the story. Share with classmates. Explain the context for each use.

5. What verb tense should be used today for Josh taking his lamb to the altar of sacrifice?

6. What verb tense should be used today for Jesus' sacrifice on the altar at Calvary?

7. What verb tense should be used for approaching the "mercy seat" today?

8. Find 12 adjectives in the Sanctuary and explain what they describe. Then find the definition for each adjective. Then write a synonym and an antonym for each adjective.

9. Collaborate with a classmate to create a poem from looking at the picture on the cover of the book "An Invitation To The Sanctuary."

10. Reread the story and list up to 10 adverbs that the author used. Use those adverbs to create a paragraph.

11. List 20 Nouns/7 Proper Nouns from the story and compose sentences with each.

12. Locate the words in the Glossary in this book. Choose one word starting with letters from (A – V) and write a sentence in your journal. Share the sentences with a classmate.

BIBLE & READING COMPREHENSION STRATEGIES TO BUILD CRITICAL THINKING:

1. Compare and contrast Mark's attitude before he met Jesus with his attitude after he met Jesus in the Most Holy Place. How can you identify in both instances?

2. Identify two cause and effects illustrations in Mark's story before his encounter with Jesus or after.

3. Summarize Mark's experience starting with his journey to the Most Holy Place.

4. Analyze the main character in the story. Explain why you like him or why you do not like him. Explain what you would change about Mark.

5. Analyze Mark's mother in the story. Explain what you liked about Mark's mother.

6. What does Mark's mother have in common with your mother or guardian?

7. Mark's father died and that impacted his life. However, his mother called on God who is a Father, to help Mark. Did God answer her prayer to help Mark? How can you encourage or pray for a classmate, a neighbor, a church member, a stranger who lost their father? Find someone and help them to see God/Jesus as their Father. Let them know how much Jesus loves them. Invite them to the "mercy seat."

8. Read your favorite chapter or other parts from "An Invitation To The Sanctuary" and create a list of all the words that rhyme with: imprecise, tenderness, ipod, leaven, feast, acronychous, chronically, incredible, infeasible, respondent, immense, prudence, remnant, emanate, and confounded.

9. Consult a dictionary to find the definition of each rhyming pair. Then use each word in a sentence, in your speaking conversation both in and out of school, and in your written communication.

BIBLE & READING - STORY STRUCTURE
GROUP SPECIAL NEEDS STUDENTS WITH ENCOURAGING PARTNERS.

1. What is the title of the story?

2. Who is the author?

3. What genre is this story? Fiction, non-fiction, realistic-fiction, Christian-fiction, religious, etc.

4. How did the setting change throughout the story-"An Invitation to the Sanctuary"?

5. Who is the main and secondary characters in the story?

6. What is the main idea of the story?

7. What was the problem/conflict in the story?

8. How was the problem/conflict resolved?

9. Who is telling the story?

10. Do the characters in the story represent anyone in real life?

11. Is there anything in the story that really happened in the past?

12. Is there anything in the story that is happening now?

13. Is there anything in the story that will happen in the future?

14. What are the major events in the story in sequential order?

15. How can you relate to these events?

16. Did any of the events remind you of something in your life?

17. What was the mood of the story at the beginning?

18. What was the mood of the story at the ending?

19. What caused the mood of the story to change from beginning to end?

BIBLE & READING-AUTHOR'S PURPOSE
GROUP SPECIAL NEEDS STUDENTS WITH ENCOURAGING PARTNERS.

1. Why do you think the author wrote this story?

2. Do you think the Bible helped to inspire the author? How do you know?

3. Does the author care about students with disability or those who have special learning needs? How do you know?

4. Based on the author's inclusiveness of different people with different abilities, will that help you to invite all people to meet with Jesus in the Most Holy Place?

5. Do you think the topic of the story is very important to the author? Why?

6. Was the author trying to persuade, inform or entertain you? How do you know?

7. What message did the author want you to get/understand?

8. Why did the author choose the specific settings for this story?

9. What did the author do to help you to visualize yourself in the various parts of the story?

10. If you could meet the author, what would you tell her? What would you like to know?

BIBLE & WRITING

EXPLORE PARTS OF A LETTER:

Friendly letter – Heading, Date, Greeting, Body, Closing, and Signature.
Business letter – Heading (return address), Date, Inside address (address you're sending to), Greeting/Salutation, Body, Closing, and Signature.

1. Write a letter to Jesus sharing your gratitude for His work in the heavenly Sanctuary on your behalf.

2. Special needs students: write or do an audio recording thanking Jesus for including you in His invitation to "come to the mercy seat." Thank Him for all that He has done for you and tell Him what you will do to share with others (those who have disability and those who do not).

3. Write a paragraph expressing what the Sanctuary means to you. Explain that a paragraph is made up of two or more complete sentences that supports one main idea.

4. List five sensory details in the story (What you could see, touch, hear, smell, taste). Describe how the sensory imagery helped you to understand the story.

5. Write a letter to the author telling how the story impacted your life or the life of others you shared with. Invite the author to your school to share.

6. Letters can be sent via email or postal mail.

7. Write a note to a friend telling what you learned about Jesus' work in the Most Holy Place.

8. Write a note of encouragement to a person with special needs (wheelchair, blindness, speech, or someone who is different than you based on a disability) tell that person that Jesus is inviting him/her to the Sanctuary so they can "experience His love." Join with another classmate to discuss how each of you can invite family and friends to the Most Holy Place to receive Jesus' love and forgiveness.

BIBLE COMPREHENSION & EXPLORATION

STUDENTS MAY SHARE ONLINE POSTS REGARDING THE QUESTIONS AND ANSWERS BELOW.

1. Compare what the Sanctuary was like in Josh's experience to what the Sanctuary was like in Mark's experience.

2. Compare Mark's response to Jesus with your own response since Jesus invites you to the "mercy seat" in the Sanctuary also.

3. What evidence can you find in the New Testament book of Hebrews chapters 8, 9 and 10 that supports the following:

- Jesus' role as High Priest and the importance of Jesus' sacrifice.

- Jesus' current location in the Sanctuary.

- That there is an original Sanctuary in Heaven.

- The two compartments of the Sanctuary and the furniture in each.

- Jesus' return after serving in the Sanctuary.

- That Jesus' sacrifice removes sin and guilt.

- That you are welcome to enter the Most Holy Place.

- What God says He will do with your sins. Based on what you found in Hebrews, what do you want to say to Jesus right now.

- Write your thoughts in your journal. Post your findings so that others can learn from you.

- Teacher: Create a special place in the classroom with a table and two chairs. Keep a Bible on the table. Allow students to go to that space to talk with Jesus in the Most Holy Place. When students need to be disciplined, gently remind them to do what Mark did in the story. He went to Jesus and confessed what he did; he apologized to his mom and those whom he hurt in school. Remind students to run to Jesus in spite of their behavior. Remind the students that Jesus calls them to "come..." in Hebrews 4:16.

BIBLE & SCIENCE IN THE SANCTUARY
STUDENTS MAY USE LIBRARY BOOKS OR ONLINE DATA TO DO RESEARCH.

... Without the shedding of blood there is no remission/no forgiveness/no release from sin and from guilt (Hebrews 9:22).

1. Assignment: Research why Jesus' blood was spotless though He was in the womb of someone who was born in sin and shaped in iniquity (Mary).

2. If someone rejects the blood of Jesus, can that person gain forgiveness for their sin?

3. Research 5 facts about blood.

4. What is the study of blood called?

5. Explain why blood is important to human existence.

6. Find out how much blood is in the human body.

7. Find out how many different types of blood there are.

8. Find out what your blood type is and memorize it. Find out if there are people (especially children) with your blood type who need a blood transfusion. How will you try to help?

9. What would happen if Jesus did not shed His blood for you and the rest of the world?

10. Write a thank you letter to Jesus for shedding His blood for you and others.

11. Illustrate how blood travels through the human body.

12. List any land or sea creatures that do not have blood.

13. Research to find out if blood comes in any other color except red. If it does, find out why.

14. Write a poem with the title: "There is Power in Jesus' Blood."

OUTREACH EVANGELISM: BLOOD DRIVE
REMEMBER TO ADVERTISE IN PERSON AND ONLINE.

1. Plan to have a blood drive at your school or church. Ask your teacher, principal and pastor to help you.

2. Contact the local agencies affiliated with the blood drives in your area.

3. Arrange the date, time and location.

4. Advertise to community, school, and church.

5. On the day of the blood drive, while people wait, share your testimony about the blood of Jesus that cleansed you from all of your sin. Explain the work Jesus did on the altar at Calvary (shedding His blood to save them). Pray with them and for those who will receive their blood.

6. Share what Jesus is doing in the Most Holy Place for them and that they are invited to the "mercy seat" also.

7. Read the entire story if they have time. Or share Mark's encounter with Jesus.

8. After asking the questions to ponder in the back of the book, ask everyone attending the blood drive if they are willing to demonstrate their acceptance of Jesus and what He did for them, what He is doing for them in the Most Holy Place right now, and what He will do upon His return.

9. Ask if they are willing to be baptized based on what they know about Jesus and continue to learn more about Jesus after baptism. Plan to stay in touch. You can study the Bible with them online.

10. Take their names, phone #, and email address.

11. Be sure to contact your principal, teacher, and your pastor to share what you want to do.

12. "Don't forget to pray before you begin" (Rowe, 2015, p. 36). Ask Jesus to touch the hearts of those who will be invited.

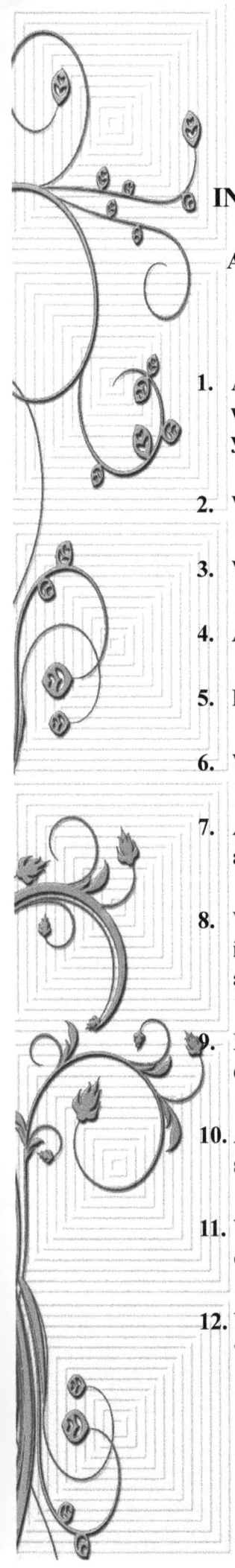

BIBLE & SOCIAL STUDIES IN THE SANCTUARY
INCLUDE TECHNOLOGY EQUIPMENT TO FACILITATE LESSONS.

As far as the east is from the west so far have I removed your sins from you. (Psalm 103:12).

1. Assignment: research how the distance can be determined between the east and the west. Explain why you think God used east and west as the distance He will remove your sin from you instead of north and south.

2. What are some of the land masses between east and west on the map?

3. What are some of the oceans between east and west on the map?

4. Are there any continents between east and west?

5. Do you or anyone you know live in the east or west of your community?

6. What does the sun do in the east and west of the sky?

7. Assignment: Research to find out where Moses built the copy of the heavenly Sanctuary. Is that place being used for something else today?

8. Was there anything in the Sanctuary from the courtyard to the Most Holy Place that is located on the east and west? (see Numbers 2 and "An Invitation to the Sanctuary")

9. MICAH 7:19 "He will again have compassion on us; He will tread our iniquities underfoot. You will cast all our sins into the depths of the sea."

10. Assignment: Research the name of the deepest sea. Find out how deep is the deepest sea. Where is the deepest sea located on the map?

11. Why do you think that God used the imagery of the depths of the sea to describe the distance that your sin will be removed from you?

12. What comparisons can you make between the "east and west" analogy and the "depths of the sea" analogy regarding the issue of sin?

OUTREACH EVANGELISM: INVITATION TO JESUS
REMEMBER TO ADVERTISE IN PERSON AND ONLINE.

PLAN AN OUTREACH EVANGELISTIC EFFORT INVITING OTHERS TO LEARN ABOUT THEIR ROLE IN THE SANCTUARY MESSAGE.

1. Copy the picture of Jesus giving the invitation in the back of the book "An Invitation to the Sanctuary." You have the author's permission.

2. On the other side of the picture, write or print your words for the invitation.

3. Your event could be during story hour on a special evening with family members, teachers, community friends and church members, an evening at church, during a few days or week of revival.

4. Remember to include the time, date, and place to meet.

5. You can do this with other classmates as a group, with family at home, with children in your sabbath school, pathfinder club, adventurer club, or just start your own "An Invitation to the Sanctuary" club!

6. When people arrive, you can share your testimony of how "An Invitation to the Sanctuary" helped you. Then you can share the story in the book with them.

7. After asking the questions to ponder in the back of the book, ask everyone attending your event if they are willing to demonstrate their acceptance of Jesus and what He did for them, what He is doing for them in the Most Holy Place right now, and what He will do upon His return.

8. Ask if they are willing to be baptized based on what they know about Jesus and continue to learn more about Jesus after baptism.

9. Take their names, phone #, and email address. Plan to stay in touch. Create a schedule with a block of time 10-15 minutes to share online Bible study questions about Jesus.

10. Be sure to contact your principal, teacher, and your pastor to share what you want to do.

11. Don't forget to pray before you begin" (Rowe, 2015, p. 36). Ask Jesus to touch the hearts of those who will be invited.

BIBLE & ARTS IN THE SANCTUARY
INCORPORATE TECHNOLOGY EQUIPMENT.

1. Draw the sanctuary scene with the Holy place and the Most Holy Place with all the furniture and the High Priest. Draw a picture of Jesus holding you.

2. Design a copy of the Sanctuary starting with the altar of sacrifice to the Most Holy Place. It can be a digital model, paper, or other materials.

3. Draw a picture showing people of every culture gathering to meet with Jesus in the Most Holy Place.

4. Make sure to use it to witness to others.

5. Look at the golden color of the Sanctuary in the Most Holy Place. Use that color to create something special for someone you never met. You can make a yellow post card/greeting card to share with people at the nursing home. Remember to include an invitation to Jesus and how much He loves them. Create yellow hearts to share with everyone you meet for at least seven days; it could be in person or online in different posts; your yellow heart must tell others about the love of Jesus. Write a whole journal entry in yellow using only positive words. Send yellow encouragement hearts to different people in your school, church and community.

6. Create yellow roses, yellow sunflower, a yellow quilt with different pieces of student contributed yellow cloth. Hang the quilt in the classroom to remind you of the welcoming place in the Sanctuary.

7. For a class art-treat: Ask all the students to bring yellow fruits and vegetables to class. Create edible art and share with students in other classes.

8. Contact and collaborate with a local artist to come to your school and teach your class how to paint. Handpaint your drawings of the furniture in the Holy Place and in the Most Holy Place of the Sanctuary.

INCLUSIVE LESSON PLAN FORMAT	
DATE:	SUBJECTS INTEGRATED:
LESSON 1, 2, 3, 4, 5, 6, 7, 8, 9, 10, OF ____ LESSONS	
Lesson Unit	LESSON TITLE:
Standard Alignment:	
Objectives/Instructional Outcomes: Outline the concept, knowledge, skill or application the students can demonstrate upon completion of this lesson. Example: there may be questions students should be able to answer, a skill students should be able to improve or perfect, or a concept student should be able to grasp and apply to various aspects of their life outside of the classroom.	
Cohesiveness in the Unit: Explain how this lesson supports the overall goal to build understanding. Explain how this lesson reinforces the concepts in the previous lesson. Explain how this lesson will provide reinforcement for the upcoming lessons.	
Materials/Resources: List all materials and resources that the teacher and students need for this lesson to be successful. Example: Prayer, textbooks, Bible, tech equipment, social studies & science supplies, expert visitor on the subject, a field trip.	
What Instructional Strategies will you use to ensure a Successful Lesson? Example: Multiple Intelligence, Centers for research/exploration, Readiness Questions to spark interests, Multi-level Mini assignment.	
Note any misconceptions you believe students may have about the subject or concept and how you plan to address them:	
List the terminology and concepts that will facilitate student's understanding to meet the objectives and the standards of the lesson & Special Needs Goal if different.	
Lesson Introduction:	
Lesson Activities:	
Questioning techniques, Grouping strategies, Teaching method.	
Lesson Closure:	
Questioning, Multi-level Mini assignment individual or group, Other demonstration of Skills learned.	
Differentiated Instruction: State how you will integrate the various needs (cultural, linguistic, IEP & other) throughout the lesson to ensure that each child experience success.	
Assessment: State the appropriate assessment for each student or group. Example: portfolio & rubrics, tests, projects & rubrics, Multi-level Mini or other assignments.	

STUDENT ACCOUNTABILITY CONTRACT FOR LEARNING

Student: *Important: (Parents Must Sign this Form for All Choices)

1. I am choosing a topic that I find interesting, that I want to know more about or that will help me to contribute to an ongoing discussion/conversation in school or outside of school.
2. I am completing a teacher-assigned project.

My Name: _____

Today's Date: _____

My Topic: _____

Type of Project: _____

I Plan to Share My Presentation Using One or Multiple Media: _____
_____

For My Project to be Exceptional, I need the following resources: _____
_____

Due Date for My Project: _____

Student Agreement: I will need _____ minutes, hours, days, weeks to complete my project. I will exercise self- control to remain focus. I will pray and ask Jesus to help me with this project because He wants me to be successful.

Student Signature: _____ Date: _____

Teacher Agreement: I will pray that Jesus helps you to complete this project successfully. I will encourage you throughout the process, provide available resources, provide verbal or written feedback as needed. I want you to be successful.

Teacher Signature: _____ Date: _____

Parent Agreement: I will pray for my child. I will do my best to provide the necessary resources for the completion of this assignment. I will monitor my child's time and be available to help him/her.

Parent Signiture: _____ Date: _____

STUDENT ACCOUNTABILITY SELF-EVALUATION FOR LEARNING
Student circle one: *Important: (Parents Must Sign this Form for All Choices)

1. I completed my project and will submit this accountability self-evaluation to my teacher.
2. I need more time for completion. (Only complete name, date topic, and project type).
3. I am exiting this project for a grade of zero. (Only complete name, date topic, project type & Parents name).

My Name: _____ Date: _____

My Topic Choice: _____

Type of Project: _____

I completed and shared my project using one or multi-media format. (10 points) _____

I followed all the criteria outlined in the rubrics provided by my teacher. (8 points) _____

I practiced self-control especially in time management. (12 points) _____

I presented my project to an audience/multiple audience. (10 points) _____

Reflection: When I started this project, I knew/ did not know_____
_____

As I gathered information, I learned _____
_____
_____

The completion of this project taught me _____
_____

I learned more about myself and others. Explain: _____
_____
_____

I also learned some new skills/vocabulary that will help me in school and other places. Explain: _____
_____
_____

*Parents/Guardians Name: _____ Date: _____

*Teacher Name: _____ Date: _____

WORKSHEET FOR BOOK: "AN INVITATION TO THE SANCTUARY"

INTEGRATED SUBJECTS: BIBLE & _____

NAME: _____ **DATE:** _____

_____
_____
_____
_____
_____
_____
_____
_____
_____
_____
_____
_____
_____
_____
_____
_____
_____
_____

WORKSHEET FOR BOOK: "AN INVITATION TO THE SANCTUARY"

GRAPHIC ORGANIZER

INTEGRATED SUBJECTS: BIBLE & _____

NAME: _____ **DATE:** _____

One: _____

Both one & two: _____

Two: _____

WORKSHEET FOR BOOK: "AN INVITATION TO THE SANCTUARY"

BIBLE & FRIENDLY LETTER WRITING

NAME:_____   DATE:_____

WORKSHEET FOR BOOK: "AN INVITATION TO THE SANCTUARY"

BIBLE & BUSINESS LETTER WRITING

NAME:_____   DATE:_____

WORKSHEET FOR BOOK: "AN INVITATION TO THE SANCTUARY"

PLANNING OUTREACH EVANGELISM: BLOOD DRIVE

NAME:_____   DATE:_____

WORKSHEET FOR BOOK: "AN INVITATION TO THE SANCTUARY"

PLANNING OUTREACH EVANGELISM: LEADING OTHERS TO JESUS

NAME:_____ DATE:_____

Name of interested person or family:_____
Email address:_____
Phone number:_____**Best time to call** _____

What can my classmates and I do to help you?

AN EDUCATOR'S PRAYER
BY: DIANA ROWE©

Dear Lord,

Please enable me to teach with Your wisdom,
Because I am working with the minds that only You can read.

Please equip me to teach with Sympathy,
Because every child needs Your compassion.

Please embolden me to teach with the love of God,
Because all my students need to experience unconditional love.

Please strengthen me to teach with grace,
Because some of my students need a second, third, fourth, and fifth chance.

Please empower me to teach with kindness,
Because many of my students do not know what kindness is.

Please help me to teach with a mind like Jesus,
Because I am literally changing the world one student at a time.

In Jesus' name,
Amen

TEACHER'S NOTES

www.ingramcontent.com/pod-product-compliance
Lightning Source LLC
Chambersburg PA
CBHW061150010526
44118CB00026B/2928